STICK, HOOK, AND A PILE OF YARN

Mervyn Seivwright writes to balance social consciousness and poetry craft for humane growth. A nomad from a Jamaican family, born in London, England, who left for America at age ten, and now residing in Schopp, Germany. Mervyn completed an MFA at Naslund-Mann Graduate School of Writing and has appeared in AGNI, Salamander Magazine, African American Review, and 56 other journals across six countries, receiving recognition as a 2021 Pushcart Nominee & 2021 Voices Israel's Rose Ruben Poetry Competition Honorable-Mention.

PRAISE for *Stick, Hook, and a Pile of Yarn*:

In *Stick, Hook, and a Pile of Yarn*, Mervyn Seivwright takes readers on a profound journey through his first encounters with America, crafting a poetry collection that is both captivating and thought-provoking. Seivwright's powerful verses vividly depict his experiences as a Black boy and man in the heart of the Midwest, offering a poignant exploration of identity, cultural assimilation, and the complexities of family dynamics. Seivwright skillfully intertwines his personal narrative with broader cultural references, from John Wayne westerns to Scarface movies. Seivwright references American icons like John Wayne and Scarface, highlighting the ongoing fascination the West has with violence and power. Seeing the West through the eyes of young Seivwright, punctuates just how complicated American culture is and how potentially violent it is, especially when seen through the eyes of a young child witnessing it for the first time. Seivwright's introspective musings also delve into the struggles of growing up with a temperamental stepfather and the struggle it was to find one's place in a blended family. His heartfelt reflections on wearing plain jeans and t-shirts while others don stylish Filas, Chuck Taylors, and Shell Top Adidas offer poignant insights into the weight of social expectations. Amid it all, Seivwright's poetic prowess shines as he describes crafting "poetic love notes" for girls and wrestling with the intricacies of love and self-discovery. Yet, within these pages lies a resounding message of resilience and hope— ending with a father's earnest plea to his son not to succumb to anger in the face of injustice, but instead to persevere and rise above any and all adversity he will face as a young Black man. *Stick, Hook, and a Pile of Yarn* is a remarkable collection that I had difficulty letting go of when I reached the final page. Through his masterful command of language, Seivwright delivers a powerful work that encourages readers to view the world from the lens of a person who sometimes felt as if he was on the margin rather than the center.

— Angela Jackson-Brown, *When Stars Rain Down*

Seivwright has written an absorbing bildungsroman that meditates on what it means to be male and Black with cultural and spiritual homes in America, Europe, and Jamaica. These poems address familial relationships, personal challenges, and triumphs, but they also expand into something greater than the self, allowing us to see power, race, and resilience, in surprising ways.

— Crystal Wilkinson, *Perfect Black*, NAACP Image Award Winner in Poetry

Stick, Hook, and a Pile of Yarn

Mervyn Seivwright

Broken Sleep Books

ISBN: 978-1-915760-34-0

Cover designed by Aaron Kent & Joe Kent

Edited & Typeset by Aaron Kent

Broken Sleep Books Ltd
Rhydwen
Talgarreg
Ceredigion
SA44 4HB

Broken Sleep Books Ltd
Fair View
St Georges Road
Cornwall
PL26 7YH

Contents

I

Manhood's Gambit	9
Stick, Hook, and a Pile of Yarn	10
Iceland, Her Touch of America	12
Three Winters - First Winter in America	13
Foreign Objects	16
No Longer in Ipswich, My Cold Quiet Place	17
First Highway Drive in America	18
Dodging Spoken Spears	19
Midwestern Gaze	20
What A Child Sees	22
The Voice of Her Work	24
Nine Months in Midwest Wheat Country —	26
My Steps Were Lost in His Path	27
My Thirteen-Year-Old Job	28
Mother's First Absence	30

II

Three Winters - Winter of Adolescence Eve	33
Just A Boy	36
If He Used His Words	38
Chilling at the Sports-O-Rama Roller Rink	39
Ignorance Still Inherits Attention —	41
School Memories	42
Ice Pusher Cream Man	44

Cracks and Canyon   45

Tickets, Tickets, Tickets   46

The Mushroom Cloud   47

The Core of the Divide   48

My Safe Bass Drum   50

Innocent Escapades   51

Late School Bus   54

Elegy to Alex   55

Chess Piece Patterns   56

III

Three Winters - Winter of Adolescence   **59**

An Assault Rifle Ode   62

An Unforgotten Path   64

From Athens to Tellico, Tennessee   65

Black Adolescent Grind   66

A Reverberant Lesson   69

Moments for a Legacy   70

Stains of His Memory   72

Each Time I Was Pulled Over   73

A Man's Demons   74

Nine Nights   76

First Time in Jamaica   77

Lessons to Unprivileged   78

Acknowledgments   81

I

Manhood's Gambit

We do not choose the parents who birthed us.

My father asked me if I wanted to stay in England.
His voice echoed between mountains with great canyons, fading,
remembering his face from two pictures, hardly,
remembering the Cadbury Roses, the aftertaste. No
loving calls, nor weekly, monthly visits recalled ever. No
proclivity for me to be rooted to his tree or spring buds.

My stepfather was present, postured to parent us with anger
instead of teaching math, football, manhood. Feeling empty
for a patriarch-guide, providing stories of life. My mummy scraping
for our emotional needs; his loving touch missing,
given to glasses of stiff drinks.

My adolescence welcomed advisement from a man, arms wide,
my friend's father, pseudo-father role teaching me
the mechanics of cars, life, to touch a woman
with respect, kind voice, a smile willing to laugh
with sincere heart.

I played the three-shell game, guessing
after a green pea, finding stale
affinity in fathers, strangers,
to explain my hairs growing, leaving reeking odors
when not cared for—my teenage feelings,
my unraveling when seized on by riotous peers,
those tempting serpents that a father or mentor
could have deflected.

Stick, Hook, and a Pile of Yarn

provided my mummy the crochet tools
she needed to thread webbed knots
years past her death. A slipknot around the hook
wrapped the yarn in knots compressed in shapes
four-sided, contrasting rainbow colours.
Yarn reading the storyline of her son, looped

around the stick. My mummy laced loops
using a stick to guide the path to come, a tool
navigating a foreshadowed path—knots
to come. Each chapter broken in hooked
pages, a marriage questioned brought shapes
in daunting dark blended colours.

Our family was far where our dusk colours
were their dawn. A variegation of seasons looped
in assent, a kidney transplant, a promise the precise tool
may not work. Mummy stitched shapes with knots
in my blanket. Knotted husband hooked
on drugs hid from his blended family. Abused shapes

came in leaves, powders, crystalized shapes
in darken green, white, tarnished yellow colours.
Mummy never read the braille shapes around the loops
of the blanket. She created a Celtic shield, a tool
to protect her son from the social vultures, knots
tightening, unraveling around him, hooked

to a path weaving him from gunshots, hooked
fish in Homestead's swamps. Mummy crocheted shapes
short of symmetry, her garden of herbs amid bark coloured
roots, sewn early before boiling sun. Flowers looped
around a tree, prism's reflection created with a small tool
for a son to harvest her joy between the knots

of a path without streetlights. My mummy knotted
her heart in the blanket, a life connected, hooked
her presence to me when she spoke no more. Diamond shapes
embedded in the blanket's centre, lighted her sun colours
letting her son know he was precious—looping
her love wrapped her warmth around him. A compass tool

of direction, a tool secured by knots my mummy
stitched guided by a hook. Stages mapped in four-sided shapes
forecasting chapters in colours, coupled in her loops.

Iceland, Her Touch of America

She did not whisper her winds—
she traversed them clutching

onto my steps—slowing my pace,
focusing my eyes to her frozen

tundra. My time with her, sunset
to sunrise, watching her fingers

find a brush—painting yellow
gleaming strokes against dark

canvas sky. Her snow swirls, floating
waves pulling as river's undertow—

waist deep—an ice ocean wasteland,
feeling of isolation, crystalizing

camera images, crackling skin,
cold cutting through seams

of layered clothes. She warned me
of the America I would find leaving her.

Three Winters - *First Winter in America*

I.

A chameleon's
instinct lives separately
on its own pathway;
journeying as a snowflake
leaving the cloud—reforming.

II.

My memories drift only to mother's family, unity
of a community, far from its Jamaican home. Morality,

our cornerstone, a foundation never questioned right
nor wrong. Loyalty is masonry that bricks our bloodline

together. Iceland's embedded ice pins, shivering insight
in America while family leagues across an ocean left

blood clots to warm my isolation. As a birthed
chameleon, I was pressed into a branch, slithering,

crawling away from the roots of the tree that ground me.

III.

"Washington, March 30 -- President Reagan was shot in the chest today by a gunman, apparently acting alone, as Mr. Reagan walked to his limousine after addressing a labor meeting at the Washington Hilton Hotel. The White House press secretary and two law-enforcement officers were also wounded by a burst of shots."
The New York Times, 30 March 1981

America celebrated cowboys. John Wayne
and Clint Eastwood were icons painting
blue, white, and red blood
for justice.

An assassin acting alone sought
justice from a Hollywood icon after studying
a Hollywood training video.

America scared me. Excited
in a country entangled in social layers I would not understand.
The first New Years at my step-grandmother's house,
the family watched Scarface and pointed guns
in the air, outside the front door—fired shots, not fireworks
with each gun in the house.

A wall of transparent celebration
and warning.

Foreign Objects

Two-week immigrants in America—
my brother and I had Suffolk accents

formed by England's east coast—new in-law
cousins introduced us to Goulds. South

of Miami, Chocolate City called by many,
a mixture of low-income housing, public

housing, drugs in housing neighborhood new
to us. We were the neighborhood's body virus,

foreign objects attacked by black blood cells.

Three boys on bicycles unwrapped a chain
from a bicycle seat-post then circled us. Our clothes,

voices, actions not appearing as anyone
they knew with the same skin—they attacked us,

swinging chain to tame fresh slaves
to condition our behavior. Dimming

our hope, twisting phrase—*Home to be brave*,
immigrants wrestling white, black blood cells.

No Longer in Ipswich, My Cold Quiet Place

Ipswich, a cold quiet place, dim earth tones, except the green
and cream buses. In Miami, a haunting heat cracked my cold

weathered skin. The sun's glare, baked leatherette seats in a vinyl-top
Chevrolet Impala, driving on six-lane streets along elongated cars—

loud bass booming music—drowned out voices. It felt like an island
movie set, chained palm trees on street corners. I saw bright prism

colors painted on a place called Burger King. The first time
I had Burger King, strawberry shake, fries, a burger—bizarre

juicy, greasy flavours consumed me. I saw spaces between buildings,
shopping centres, houses with long olive flapping butterfly leaves

on banana trees. I saw trees of fresh lemons, mangoes, oranges,
starfruits. I was in the place of stars—cowboys, gangsters, Kung Fu

movies. The place where on television, everybody was shooting.
The place where voices twang like long guitar notes in the sun.

First Highway Drive in America

Driving in America passing palm trees,
Florida's grassy green marshlands,
counting mile-markers in the rear seat
of a gray station wagon with my brother.
He and I navigating a map
longer than our arms, playing
magnetic checkers and chess, reading,
counting red cars, navigating

again. Across the Georgia border, dirt
is dusty red on hills edging fields
of floating cotton. The radio in Atlanta
reports that 19 black boys and girls
our age was missing or dead. We navigated

our car without ceasing across
the Georgia-Tennessee line. A Big Boy
restaurant wasn't as friendly as the statue
with static wave and smile out front. Entering
the door, a stage curtain opens,
ninety-four eyes fixate—our family
stops at the entrance scared from the shadow
on our skin.

Dodging Spoken Spears

"I know what you want for Christmas" echoes—internally bled tears.
A six-year-old child brings cute smile without front teeth,
my adolescent journey played hide and seek, dodging spoken spears.

I regret being a child, playing war in a darken room full of chairs
Flipping, hitting my adult tooth broken—kids chanted taunts growing grief—
"I know what you want for Christmas" echoes—internally bled tears.

Dentist had me wait until my teeth had matured the following years,
jokes raining, "Toothless, can you eat through the hole", brought disbelief—
my adolescent journey played hide and seek, dodging spoken spears.

Moving to America I could leave the "Gap" echoes, I puzzled peers
with my foreign accent; the gapped face poured mockery after short relief—
"I know what you want for Christmas" echoes—internally bled tears.

I limited myself to cloaked corners, not to play—social shame flourish fears,
I limited public displays, spoke sparsely, learned to smile not showing teeth—
my adolescent journey played hide and seek, dodging spoken spears.

Each place we moved, each different school, each area I appeared
used Pony Express messages, spreading this song sung as motif,
"I know what you want for Christmas" echoes—internally bled tears,
my adolescent journey played hide and seek, dodging spoken spears.

Midwestern Gaze

Our basement was my play haven
under a thousand-square-foot
home—my get-a-way space
from my brother, parents.

In our basement I mimicked
an English footballer shooting
goals with a foam football
against a chalk drawn goal

on the wall. My mummy fleeted
downstairs carrying radio,
blankets, pillows to place on cold
cement floor, scurried for vital

documents, pictures, cherished
family collectables. My family
hauled folding chairs, drinks,
snacks down to my basement

playground, theatre, stadium.
Mummy shouted we had to shelter.
I jetted upstairs without a care,
without fear—rushed out the door,

saw it swirling, wind churned
towards us. Seven streets away
tornado grabbing loose clouds,
toys, tree limbs in its funnel.

Facing danger fuels a ten-year old's
interest—I drown out my mummy's
screams to retreat downstairs—hypnotized
my eyes gawked as it calmed to a whisper.

What A Child Sees

Children do not receive
the cause—children see

the effects. Christmas
at nine, an American
military man
in England,
we would call
stepfather gave us plentiful
presents; gave mum
security when she worked
at night, taking my brother
and I to see *Convoy*, doubled
with X-rated movie,
visions that brought
a nine-year old
unease.

By eleven, in America
I received pitiful
presents. He connected
to us with food. Fishing
at local lakes
and rivers, hours
on weekends
eating overfished
schools of bluegill
too small. Shot a rock
with his slingshot
killing a robin, furry
idolized robin falling
to thump off telephone

wire outside our home;
deep fried it, telling me
it tasted like chicken,
choking up
when he made me taste.

Our house
was much smaller—
finances depleting—
Tequila, beer, and Cognac's
rent was paid
in our home.
Mummy had two jobs—
we rarely saw her. I felt
inside mummy
was happy. I was taught
to be seen, a limpid chameleon,
silent observations, invisible.
Knots in a crocheted
blanket, a braille language
taking years to read.

The Voice of Her Work

My mummy was a nurse's aid
in England. In Iowa, her skills
did not translate: one uniform
split into two. Stories of where
she worked spoken
from the uniforms
left at home lingering
to layered rings of stains,
darkening my mummy`s joy—
diminishing her first visions
of Hollywood America.

Mornings her night uniform
told me about the infused sweet,
sticky, syrup next to steak
and bacon juices on brown Perkins' apron
left from cleaning after truckers,
before their midnight drive. Decorative
eggs and avocado paint on mummy`s
skirt highlighted by the white gravy
from crack of dawn officers off-shift.
Her pockets filled with pennies, quarters,
a few crimpled paper-bills soaked in coke

stains—tips mirroring her service. Evenings
her day uniform serviced seeped up coke
dust, dripped red wine
and coffee drizzling off the table edges,
blended on ruffles of her Days Inn
tan and cream dress. Uniform
became a mixing flask, floating aroma
with Ajax, bleach, Comet, turpentine

and vinegar bringing dizzy spells, causing
cloth-hem bloats fading from scrubbing
missed toilet-urine splatter, condom
cum blotches left from hourly stay
club-lovers with lost memories of shame.

Nine Months in Midwest Wheat Country—

amber grains wave in Des Moines, silence
the s—the monks have left. Just above
poor-trash-class life, south-side, struggling.
America. Our neighbor accepted us,

we play his Mattel's Intellivision
video game. Watch him run outside
to grab softball size hail, storming
winds in circles, innings of pitches
from the sky. We listen to Music
Television's birth: "Video Killed
the Radio Star," "In the Air Tonight,"
"Stop Draggin' My Heart Around,"

"Whip it." We went scrapping
for spare change, cutting grass,
collecting glass bottles. Joy riding,
jumping bikes in hilly dunes,
four-wheelers across sandy dunes,
jeeps in curvy dunes—hanging on
to jeep rails as the jeep rolls over—night joy
finds us tipping tired cows over—
hiding in shadows from angry farmers.

My voice places me in speech classes
so my American teacher can understand
my English accent. Not sure if I got picked
on being black, sounding different,
or not being American when a car passed
our car with a sign, "*Niggers kiss ass*",
squeezing ass cheeks against passenger
window. Amber grains wave us away.

My Steps Were Lost in His Path

Family said I would inherit my uncle's ways.
At age eight I didn't have his swag;
medium seventies afro, top named clothing,
sleek pointed shoes, clean, ironed button-down

shirt, chiseled face on dark Jamaican man.
He was a loyal protector of family
who found his own path in the world. Easy

to see how a young nephew remembered
the charisma that oozed in his uncle's presence—
as I did. We left England years before word

of his arrest. I heard stories in mummy's phone
calls about uncle's lavish lifestyle, ominous
guise. I acted out, poor grades and discipline

when left in America for the first time.
She departed to bury her brother,
who somehow killed himself, never

part of his demeanor to be insecure,
to feel shame in his stride, to slay himself.
My mummy sensed the truth walking

between mortar and metal prison space—
hands of another put him in final sleep, story
that lies dormant between cold prison walls.

My Thirteen-Year-Old Job

Sunday mornings would be the most work—
in Syracuse, New York, snow packed

in stacks sometimes several feet high
so riding a bicycle could only be used

distributing our summer supply, but
this was February with fresh snow.

My brother and I would be pulled by a fish-
line tug from sleep, eager for the four a.m.

knock at our door. Answering quickly, not
allowing our parents to wake. Our distributor

already had stacks of Sunday newspapers
to hand us before returning to his truck

for more. More as Sunday newspapers
have weekly coupons, weekly sports stats,

weekly social events, and gossip. People
unable to roll over from sleep to reach

for phone's highlights, no digital media,
just media in fresh pressed ink. Established

Sunday as the day of the week for news,
a paper seven folds thicker than the rest.

We would have to pack the stacks of newspapers
with coupons, distributed in separate

stacks that took an hour prior to packing
the stacks of newspapers tied down on snow

sleds. We dressed in wrapped layers
to stay warm, flexible enough to attack

the street in strategic patterns by six a.m. We
were snow dogs mushing the neighborhood

streets. Newspapers were too thick to throw,
and could not be blended with snow, so

we placed newspapers behind screen doors
with quiet precision. Quiet enough

that dogs in homes stayed sleep, not waking
owners or conducting the howling canine

neighborhood choir. Allowing us to swish
silently in the snow back home to sleep.

Mother's First Absence

My mother flew to England to bury
her brother—five weeks without her,
only my stepfather, my brother left at home.
I rebelled as a tween letting lazy behavior
fail middle school midterm grades

in each class. My mother never left us
brothers this long—never left us in the hands
of an abusive tongue, aggressive triggered
man with alcoholic tendencies.

My mother was the one who physically punished
us. Each midterm failure I gave my stepfather
angered him to belch out, *It's your ass*
for anymore. Cringing my face with silence
to solitude, hooked to my bedroom. One midterm
form left—fearing his threat of heavy hands, tearing
through our telephone book for child abuse

hotline. I repeated the phone number
whispered in my breath between pauses
of dark dream sleep, the length of morning
bus ride to school, numbers spiraling
specific intention spiked fear in return.

II

Three Winters - *Winter of Adolescence Eve*

I.

I thought America was ink
on paper. Not letters combined
and shaped to shake emotions,

communicate messages, sing
stories. I felt like the unplanned
ink blotches before a pen dies

staining fingers. Each school
away from a city, cultivated
ink blotches, black children

stretched across paper
spaces. Our eyes finding
each other in horizons
of light. Our eyes voicing

togetherness, not allowing us
to unite, stains on white-page disgust.

II.

'Military Brat:' Do You Know Where the Term Comes From?
"[The term "military brat] pertains to those children who grew up in military families. "Brats" wear the name like a badge of honor, often because of the moves, stressors and cultural experiences that make them more resilient than their civilian counterparts."
By Katie Lange
DoD News, Defense Media Activity

I was a base brat. Hidden
behind barbed-wire fence lines, behind
cultural hatred, behind community
differences with generations of families,
not changing, behind soldiers at gates,
protecting us. We integrated schools,
bused in and out like Southern cities
in the sixties—children baked
from America men and each painted
culture from the artist's pallet. Trained
to let parents leave—mine never
left. Never left the militant orders
at the door of our home, barking
directions, diminishing my spirit
with details of chores not perfected,
his details were left in a bottle.

III.

I wrote a declaration
to hate girls. Following
the Forefathers of the country
with John Hancock signature
centered in large print—
each boy with yucky, icky
feelings shared about girls signed
at this age, until the following
year.
       She was Italian,
green eyes, long slightly curled
ginger hair—seemed different.
I seemed different—I passed
middle school cryptic
folded notes, showing
interest without confessing
interest. I was brave
enough to hint as class hoard
sung my secrets. She smiled.
Not rejecting or sharing her
interest in me.

Leaving a yearbook note
of my departure, remember
me always—*Love Stephanie.*

Just A Boy

He was just a harmless Boy
Scout. Playing Dungeons
and Dragons in the woods,
carving detailed wooden
daggers and swords assisted
by fire, molding a sharpened
shape—architecting snow
forts, bush forts, tree forts
for hiding—startling.

He was just a curious Boy
Scout. Assessing which red
berries were edible, biting
strands of spicy Bambi
jerky—smirking, crafting
a miniature trident spear
for gigging frogs, skinning
frog legs, cooking them
in campfire stew with carrots,
secret sauce, boiling cut
French fries, not realizing
his mummy used oil.

He was just an innocent Boy
Scout. Transferring tadpoles
from river creek into scalding
pot, creating a race, swimming
for exit, swimming from
execution. Filling friends'
socks with innocuous
spiders. Pulling out tent stakes
of those still sleeping at dawn.

He was just an adventurous Boy
Scout. He cooled off
in Cayuga Lake, heating knife,
burning off wiggling leeches
latched to his skin. He
shaved wooden spikes
buried in traps camouflaged
by tall grass fields for bears
or Red Eye, a crazy woodman
with a glowing blood-shot eye.

If He Used His Words

This wouldn't be the last time he left blue packets
on our beds. Lubricated latex Durex listed
on the labels in the bedroom my brother
and I shared as early teens. No sensitive speech

from our stepfather including bees, bears, birds—
no animal springtime sprawling metaphor
of sex teaching us about our heightened hormones
or use of condoms. Maybe my stepfather

never shared this speech with his father. Maybe
my stepfather never had vulnerable flashes
with his father to harness. Maybe. His sparse conversations
with us were unilateral directing discipline. Militant orders,
echoed vulgarities—his empty echoes filled guzzled glasses
of Cognac. Expired condoms in my wallet dried.

Chilling at the Sports-O-Rama Roller Rink

Roller skating—teenage mating
ritual on Friday nights in North

Syracuse. Hormones high—shy
while stuttering words, murmuring

from my lips and trying not to trip
steps so I appeared in control. Faking

great skating on the rink, shaking
upper body enough not to lose

balance, keeping my feet steady.
Stop. Break away from the rink

to taste each flavor—drinking
suicide soda to keep sweet energy

in my gas tank. Each break
between skate periods I enter

the dance-room. Darkened space,
flickering lights with disco, pop,

soul music popping "Beat it,"
"Billie Jean," "Doctor Doctor,"

"The Wild Boys," Inferno's "Burn
Baby Burn"—sneaking cigarettes—

smoking to be cool—my virgin lungs
choking machine-gun cough—

startling teenage couples in corners,
hidden in shadows between the lights.

Ignorance Still Inherits Attention—

my 3-stripe shoes—no name, not
Filas, Chuck Taylors, Shell Top
Adidas, nor matching
Adidas sweats, Puma sweats, Nike
windbreaker, bubble vest. Humbled
in my plain jeans and t-shirt,
generated their jokes—*Yo moma so
slow, fat, ugly, dumb.* Picked at
my 3-stripe shoes—no name, not
suede Nikes, suede Pumas, suede
Ballys, nor matching fat laces,
spikes, Kangos, skullys,
parachute pants for b-boying,
or gold teeth brothers in Miami
stuck with prison pants
too big to stay on, released
to pants still big—hanging off ass
with silk shirts, Fisherman caps
watching me walk wearing
my 3-stripes shoes—they called them,
bo bo heads.

School Memories

Public prison,
eight windows
broken, boarded
up only omitting
rifle towers,
barbed wire
fences. Upon
entry appeared
metal detectors—
all students
frisked
for contraband,
not discovering
M80s hidden
under trumpet
case felt lining
from the boy
ahead of me
in this outpatient
four-year bid
high school.

First day,
not forgetting
her face, passing
in slow
hummingbird
motion, felt
her expression,
forced around
concealed corner,

blackened corner,
muscled down
resisting, desiring—
my voice stolen
to speak.

Back of school
gangs scattered
in locked
courtyard spots
boosted bundle
sales in front
of student
façade cops—
flashed badges—
flashed pace—
students scuttled,
switched clothes,
chess castling,
the boy caught,
pleaded, professed
he was a double.

Ice Pusher Cream Man

Faint wind brings the truck's familiar jingle,   foul
and sweet smells explodes joyful taste buds,   dried up buds
for children in elementary, junior high,   high school,
dripping, melting flavors of ice cream,   ice.

At this school bus stop,   exchange
children in waves get their sugar   and product
from early morning time,   late night
selling not only soft-serve ice cream,   Scat and Sauce
selling Klondike, Chipwich   and Skunk,
Strawberry Shortcake, Chocolate Éclair   and Bennies in a bunch,
Ice Cream Sandwich, Bomb Pops   and Oxy,
Drumsticks, Snow Cones   and Red birds to fly,
this wasn't an ordinary   product supply.

His attire was basic,   a wife beater vest,
rough thinned-out hair style   with cut off pants
and beer belly,   scraggy beard to his chest.
Mornings, afternoons   before school buses would show
I never heard his van jingle,   kids already planned to go
to him before the short walk home,   late getting home
and spend left over lunch change   or cash they made,
    investing   a pusher man's story,
        a capitalist paid.

Cracks and Canyon

~~I wrestled with deformities~~, my ~~teeth, stressing stone~~
~~crazing cracks, lost heart moisture, found~~ words, ~~in my fall-out shelter shielding~~
~~stinging expressions. A girl adored knew how I~~ wrestled ~~with emotions—~~
~~mistaking my words as baneful forfeit, she spoke~~ with ~~my mother;~~
~~school system stuck me in circle of~~ life ~~high-risk teenagers~~

~~outside my shelter, behind closed doors.~~ My ~~story did not reflect~~
~~gun shots, pill pops, wrist cuts. I was a~~ world ~~away from last~~
~~breath. I whispered to my counselor that~~ wrestled ~~with life. My mother,~~
~~father, family, friends crowded me~~ with ~~love. A canyon~~
~~of my confused conclusions wrestled with~~ death.

Tickets, Tickets, Tickets

Six numbers, 1 to 53.
50, 12, 8, 14, 11, 47.
My mother's birth date—his birth date
played on the lottery tickets daily
for a month. Switched birth dates
to marriage dates,
to funeral dates,
to lucky dates
on tickets. I remember

exploring their bedroom
for school lunch change. Sock drawer—
tickets. Shoe boxes—
tickets. Nightstand—
tickets. Decor sheathed in red flamingos
tickets flapping change away. Enough
to build a mansion of cards from tickets
filled an empty house, flawed
foundation, flaying winds
blowing dreams away. College dreams—

sixty-six percent of Floridians approved a lottery
for thirty-eight percent of the state educational use—
my stepfather paid for a stranger's education.
Scratch-off tickets—

coins filtering through fingers
stripping clothes away—a naked family—
dollars at a strip club
brings more seconds of sport.

The Mushroom Cloud

6 IN CREW AND HIGH-SCHOOL TEACHER ARE KILLED 74
SECONDS AFTER LIFTOFF
Thousands Watch Rain of Debris
*"Cape Canaveral, Fla. Jan. 28 -- The space shuttle Challenger exploded in a ball
of fire shortly after it left the launching pad today, and all seven astronauts on
board were lost."*
By William J. Broad
Special to *The New York Times*

Our eyes didn't leave the sky. We
were 200 miles from the space
center. On clear days we saw past launches
cloud-trails to space. On this clear day
we saw smoke, white cloud mushroom spores,
bending, speeding its growth. Chemistry
high school students standing speechless,
tearful in disbelief. Our eyes
didn't leave the sky studying the smoke
standing still—a trophy for nature,
an image imprinted to the file drawers
in our brains, clicking 8-millimeter
film-frames blacking out before the real
movie reel. Our eyes didn't leave
the sky. Our teacher did not console
us, we were stone still outside
the school, statues spread out
in a French garden, hypnotized
with a chill. Our eyes refused
to leave the sky—and them alone.

The Core of the Divide

Location was blurred once
I met her, teased by tight curves
attaching my gaze on mocha
chocolate skin, snatching shyness
finding my voice to call her. Calls
on a push button phone, speaking
the distance of a spaghetti cord
extended through my home.

Divided by a city's landscape
she seeks the core of a city
to search the core of me. Miami
streets. No taxis. No buses left
after we arrived to meet next

to palm tree scenes. Searching
for roots tangling towards each
emotion hidden behind scars
of broken promises. We walked
weaving traffic until sounds
around us were scarce. Sun

descended with our voices entangled
with crescent smiles. Desolate
streets only provide interruption
of dust scattered from sports cars
speeding under the city lights
that guided us. Cloudless night

brought cold sea-breeze short
of blanket, cold sea-breeze
froze new roots together without
a bus until morning—only a park
bench in light's dark divide found
our scents mixed; our bodies bound.

My Safe Bass Drum

I used to fall in love
a lot. Write poetic love
notes. Create mixed slow
jam tapes with voice overs—
This is for you, girl.
Draft poems with hand
drawn flowers,
and if she was friendly
singing words
in a sparrow's tune.
I'd scraped change
from my pizza job
and purchased a gold
plated heart. Waiting
to see if each one
of these Juliets weren't
scared of my Cyrano
affliction, missing two
front teeth as teenager,
not a kodak image
for Homecoming dance
memories. Blended mask
of marching band's
largest bass drum
covering me at football
games, banging out
the pain, muffle feelings
into a polyethylene
and wooden box.

Innocent Escapades

I.

Late Boxing Day had my mate and I creating
music on a Christmas keyboard, lacking
experience of keys, notes, or bars

for a song that we would write. My mother
and brother sleeping, we quietly chain
keys in melodic sounds, pleasing

our minds for a top love song inspired
by New Edition's "Lost in Love"—nerds
with nerves seeking acceptance. Tired

of crushes created scared moments crashing
to kick rocks when a girl was standing there. But
a hit song, well a nice song could balance fears.

II.

This night we seek approval from a girl
we both knew to share our idea, this song
that she could hear at a neighbor park.

We had to sneak, holding always clanging
screen door of my home and enter a gate
of the military base before midnight, before

curfew for those under eighteen had to be
home. Hormones hinder teenage thoughts
whisking between houses to this girl's home.

Out of her bedroom window she climbed
dressed in stripped sand colored night gown
just above her knees. Her house next to the park

after twelve and very dark, lost debating
about the song we created for love. She
had a cute crush on my mate, asking him

to push her swing until we saw small
orange light in the dark. The increasing
silhouette revealed a slow burning

cigarette from a military cop moving gradually
across the grass. We could not run between
the shadows of night, we were worried and in fright

from the first words spoken by this cop.
Speaking slowly, he questioned why, after
midnight we didn't comply with the curfew

rules that night. Our truth sounded like
a lie, two boys, a girl in a night gown
looked funny in the cop's eyes—*Sir,*
we said, *We were just writing a song.*

Late School Bus

The smell of foul eggs set a flame, each time

the school bus would pass this block; stench

of baked cocaine mixture, blowing aroma,

robust enough that senses were seized

when approaching a sharp bend of the route

restraining the bus to walking pace. Each child

cringed nasal intolerance before bus windows

were shut. Deep into the bend bus momentum

stringed out zombie-like people chasing, gawking

at us children, their hands hanging in drugged run

as we scurried away.

Elegy to Alex

We don't die when our name is spoken. School
is a place of life lessons whether on
a curriculum or not. Lessons lived
in reprocessed memories unless safe
door is shut.

And forgotten. Finding lines
I once wrote, "In our hearts he will stay," lost,
on my shelves. Triggering flashbacks, his kind
voice missing, a church spilling on sidewalks,
a wailing chorus, an untuned organ.

Finding lines on online blog by mother
brings to life—her baby, his poems, his
letters, my crocheted life hooked with him—not
the car that cradled his last breath. He was
our drum major, directing lives, drawing
band together to drive us, laugh, and cry.

Chess Piece Patterns

I was never taught how to play
chess. At seven, I watched

my uncle position-play his friends
after his Amway presentations.

Dimensions of strategy, stretching
my mind six moves ahead

with pyramid impact, knotted
in my memory. I learned

most people I met repeated
movements, chess pieces

within safe parameters, recurring
pawns and rooks, looped

by a yarn of life's conditions,
compelled by fear, failure—running

when others were running
without hearing the gunshots

others heard at a Miami Bass
concert. A girl is laughing

loving a boy in our high school
locker room—a train of six

boys follows. I blend
hidden against a dark corner.

III

Three Winters - *Winter of Adolescence*

I.

No two front teeth. Love
is a teenager
reaching for a golden
thread in a farm of hay.

Television writes
a biblical guide on clothes,
appearance, and social
acceptance for teenagers—
each page painting
me as a child sitting with the misfits.

Listening to kids' voices echoes of "Gap",
singing to me, "All I want for Christmas"—

Waiting for the knife
against the wrist.

II.

I was missing two front teeth. Poetry spoke for a shy face.
Faces sculpted with charisma birth feelings of ~~love~~ a crush
Euphoric feelings, mixes of paint distant from primary colors
Each face, a muse molding words what my mind could not

Faces sculpted with charisma birth feelings of love ~~a crush~~
Crushed from rejection, a dull dagger, frozen, twisted against skin
Each face, muse molding emotions that my mind could not
Confining my face in quiet corners, cloaking my teeth, disfigured

Crushed from rejection, a dull dagger, frozen, twisted against skin
Playing Freddy Jackson's, "Have you ever loved somebody?"
Confining my face in quiet corners, cloaking my teeth, disfigured
Until the next face I saw placed words on a new ~~crush~~ love on paper

Playing Freddy Jackson's, "Have you ever loved somebody?"
I blanketed my insecurity, wrapped as caterpillar in a chrysalis
Until the next face I saw placed words on a new crush ~~love~~ on paper
Emotions crocheted, weaving a pattern until concrete blanket is made

I blanketed my insecurity, wrapped as caterpillar in a chrysalis
Euphoric feelings, mixes of paint distant from primary colors
Emotions crocheted, weaving a pattern until concrete blanket is made
I was missing two front teeth. Poetry spoke for a shy face.

III.

The gap was filled. The winter
of my junior year I skipped school,
spending six weeks in England. I filled

the gap, emptiness of family—filled. I filled
the gap, a bridge connecting missing teeth. I filled
the gap, anxiousness became assurance

in the mirror. I filled the gap of past crushes
when I met her—caramel skin, straight black hair
straddling shoulders, light brown-green eyes, dancing

dancehall and reggae tunes, winding hips, touching
past words written on a page. Touching
her lips, left with smoke flavor—ignored, touching
her curves, shape outlined Vogue visions, touching

myself, lost in a written dream. I dug
a gap across an ocean leaving her—letters
swimming the ocean left long yearning;
a slipknot loosening without a hook.

An Assault Rifle Ode

1077 innocent Americans found
blooded end in mass collection.
Assault rifles held by people
with uncontrolled emotions
triggering projectiles.

An assault rifle, merely
a composition of wood,
steel, plastic or iron forged
into a projector to thrust
projectiles in rapid force.

An assault rifle cannot
be personified, no emotions,
not greed, rage, aggression,
vengeance, disgust.

An assault rifle can be an M, XM,
AR, AK, HK, bullpup, forged
by Sturm Ruger, Remington,
Savage, Smith and Wesson,
Mossberg, Heckler and Kock—
two-point-four billion in sales.

Assault rifle sales; influenced
by a country, faction, family,
person's assault or defense.

An assault rifle does not plan
and organize its constructed
purpose, hard and cold until
inflamed from embrace.

An assault rifle is a tool, held
by people feeling controlled
emotions within the law,
protecting innocent lives
from civil disobedience.

An assault rifle held by a person
I cannot see in a blue sportscar
on South Miami Street corner
with muzzle pointed at me.

An Unforgotten Path

November 18, 1987: "Fire at King's Cross Underground station leaves 31 dead"
"The worst fire in the history of the London Underground killed 31 people and injured more than 100 when a stray match started a blaze beneath a wooden escalator."
By Chas Early, *British Telecommunications*

Thirty-one scorched—one week
before I went home
to London. I was lost.
seven years since I left
my childhood in England.
My father told me
to meet at King's College,
I arrived at King's Cross
six miles away. Accosted
by roses, carnations, lilies,
a meadow of flowers
bunched in yellow, pink,
green crepe-paper bundles
amassed as a river. Baptizing
grouped onlookers, sliding
as snails sunken in pictures.
Memories were weathered
soiled, faded from sun
and rain, rinsing the newness
repeated by mothers,
daughters, sons struggling
to fill the gaps. I struggled
to fill the gaps without
my father, a fragile bond
as the crepe-paper bridging
across a great ocean—not sinking
in pictures of my father, ripping
at minuscule memories to fade.

From Athens to Tellico, Tennessee

In the summer of my late teens my best
friend's father fathered me on things I thought
men should do. Away in Athens, nested

amidst dogwood trees, fields with lavender
wildflowers, blended in green tinted meadows
in Tennessee. I learned to listen to crickets

build networks where telephones may not ring
often. A neighbor called my best friend's father's
father and asked if he had hired help.

*Just my Korean grandson and his black best
friend.* My best friend's father spoke about girls,
intimacy while driving on Tellico Mountain

roads, as each car passed, he pushed my head down,
shrouded my skin from folks with hatred for brown.

Black Adolescent Grind

I.

Raggedy Rusted Fifteen-Year Old Red Car

How many young black men should be on their knees each night?

Outside our window in a suburban neighborhood, a sea of middle to upper class fenced homes see a red car. Two o'clock in the morning, a raggedy rusted fifteen-year old car is revving in our neighborhood with four black men waking good white folks. This neighborhood, with only two black families.

How many young black men should be on their knees each night?

One raggedy rusted fifteen-year old red car with four black men; red and blue lights, a single siren rings from three saving sheriff department cars, surrounding them, demanding the four black men out of the car with hands interlocked behind their head and dropping to their knees.

II.

Coconut Grove in the Eighties

Saturday Nights in the Grove was full
of Metro-Dade police officers on each block. Full
of mixed Caribbean, Latina girls in short dresses. Full
of gangs of young men like me representing their hoods. Full
of attitudes, concealed pistols, switchblades, brass-knuckles
to defend ourselves when Metro-Dade police were not watching.

Saturday nights in the Grove at midnight
cars are chock-a-blocked—quicker to stroll the streets. At midnight
eateries were open with florescent lights, outside tables. At midnight
college students were running in rickshaws carrying couples. At midnight
streets were covered in crowds crowd-watching—hard to view our pistols,
switchblades, brass-knuckles when Metro-Dade police were not watching.

Saturday nights in Coconut Grove were toxic
waiting for a pin to be pulled from the grenade,
waiting for the wrong hand-sign-formation,
waiting for murky shadows between restaurant lamps,
eerie crackling skin, waiting for one to stop breathing.

III.

Raggedy Rusted Fifteen-Year-Old Red Car

How many young black men should be on their knees each night?

Late night concert ends during rare Floridian cold night finds us stopping
in an upscale suburban neighborhood to warm up this raggedy rusted
fifteen-year-old red car. Just traveling home, delayed by red and blue
lights, single siren ring from three surrounding police cars.

Would I ever get home this night?

Flashlights bright enough to blur faces, voices demanding us out the raggedy
rusted fifteen-year-old red car with arms raised, palms showing, fingers interlocked,
screaming *BOY* in our ears, pushing us hard to knees, scraping pants to drips
of blood, smelling road oil, grit in my mouth. My praying position seeking deliverance.

A Reverberant Lesson

Ongoing nights he shouted, shaking
me from sleep, his voice, a drunken
pirate presence, southern drag, staccato
curse-words connected by conjunctions.

Wake up, wash the dishes—dishes
from evening cleaned now placed back
in the sink stacked due to grease
spots my stepfather found—he released
me from sleep. Eyes were blurred

burning salt-drops—I used superfluous soap
suds on dishes, not to repeat my behavior,
not to repeat his behavior—his recycled
drunken discharge over the years drifted me
away from drink—sobered choices I weighed.

Moments for a Legacy

Dr. King's anniversary holiday
of life found me in an Overtown Park,
celebrating his legacy of civil disobedience,
eating conch fritters, crispy fried, soft;
counting women wearing colored weave,
counting gold teeth on men in Miami,
unaware how many would raise their voice
to holler injustice two blocks, two hours away.

> "*Clement Anthony Lloyd, the motorcyclist felled Monday by a police officer's bullet, was a husky, funny, happy-go-lucky entrepreneur who thumbed his nose at the law and left behind a girlfriend five months pregnant with his child. Allan Blanchard, who died of massive head injuries from the crash, was his quiet sidekick, a frightened newcomer to a city he found violent and unwelcoming.*"
> Christin Evans and Charisse L. Grant
> Herald Staff Writers, 18 January 1989, *The Miami Herald*, FL

Two blacks listed in headlines,
not men, fleeing from police. One
painted as a rebel with hands holding
the motorcycle. One, painted scared,
holding the rider, running late night
through Overtown for traffic violations.
Police both judge and executioner pleading
fear with gun in his hand, shot bullet
in rider's head, the other one crashed dead.

> "*The most dangerous creation of any society is the man who has nothing to lose.*"
> — James Baldwin, *The Fire Next Time*

Uncivil disobedience. Dr. King's legacy found
a city unwilling to relent, crowd confused, channeling
together, New Orleans Second Line band celebrating
a dead relationship with the city, burning cars, burning

buildings—an atom splitting fire, sparking each black hood
bringing daylight to shine on a city's neglect
of the lost. A people tired of talking, walking, boycotting
for equal treatment, tossing rocks, bottles at uniforms
that serve, tired of being nothing.

"It is a very rare man who does not victimize the helpless."
— James Baldwin, *No Name in the Street*

Each day after, a girl I knew told me her hood
was burning—city servants find their Vietnam
unable to identify friendlies, creeping
in slow groups along each side street. People
carrying couches on their back, apocalyptic
hoards stumbling around ash framed cars
smoldering mental blown smoke. People
grabbing each can of food, package of rice
from their corner stores—the girl told me
even someone snatched the purse and car
from her helpless grandmother
in her driveway.

Stains of His Memory

My mother loved the beige house with orange,
apple, kiwi, and two mango trees spread
across the backyard. Our home was in South
Miami, streets filled with loose battle-type

rottweilers and pit bulls seeking walkers
falsely secured by weak fences. This was
the neighborhood we could afford. A house
claiming safety behind bars on windows

and doors. Feeling of prison when
we could not find the keys. My stepfather
plagued with tempered emotions
lost promotions during a military

life of twenty years. Infested by drug
addiction from the Vietnam War, moments
away in Korea, finding outlets
to deal with images and pain. Still high

soaked on those images and pain—spending
days away from home after his paychecks
came from his security guard job—coming
back with ashes left. Spare change could not keep

our lights on, keep our water running, keep
our home. My mother found brandy glass
covered in aluminum foil; burnt rocks
left yellow stains in the glass. Stains

in my stepfather's memories released in smoke.

Each Time I Was Pulled Over

as a teen, I kept my credentials
and dependent ID close enough
to limit movements. My brown hands

stayed in plain sight, shifting
slowly when asked for registration,
shifting my eyes for empathy

without awareness of my fault.
Maybe to allow pity to a child
of a military man, increasing

my status or worth. A hostage
is told to humanized themselves
to a captor, be a softer skinned victim.

I softly said *yes sir*, kept my eyes
submissive, was thankful
for the ticket for not stopping

at the stop-sign, where
I had earlier stopped my car.

A Man's Demons

My stepfather could be kind
when his hidden demons
did not plague decisions I discerned.

A child can only analyze actions,
shadows reflecting the body,
motions to mimic, wrestling

with the waves causing callous
repercussions, creating chameleon
reactions from what my teen-vision

saw. I observed a man whose hands
painted mastery, Michelangelo's student
touching his canvas, one could feel

a man's face. I observed a man
whose voice was soulful enough,
a stranger debating marriage would

buy a wedding ring. I observed
when his hands weren't moving,
when the theater was empty, echoes

rose of tales he kept to himself. Voices
from the demons that plagued him
gave him his vices, filling glasses,

rising temper, spreading anger,
drinking, puffing, smoking, choking
a life, stagnating work promotions,

taking shallow steps towards goals,
a peeled banana softened, blackened,
losing firm grounding around himself.

Maybe the pressure of military life
and death darkened visions from friends
never forgotten. Maybe the pressure

of social behaviors of blended family
caused misery. Maybe the pressure—
coming to his hometown after two-decades,

finding old friends, riding the same street
corners and blocks became his framework
to live. Maybe. I still may love him; his

decisions left my mother in an unmarked grave.

Nine Nights

I was told that crying showed
a lack of faith, selfishness, a show
to shadow the truth. Nine evenings
      in remembrance, celebrating
      flashes in stories,

jokes, songs over strong drink—
Red Stripe beer, Appletons, Wrey
and Nephews rum. Nine days
      of preparation, potato, yam,
      stubborn goat stressed bleating

on all fours for our festivities—
kicking, fussing before bloodletting,
hung on hind legs, used in broth
      for mannish water at grave digging
      party, socializing each night

with band and selector—dancing,
slapping dominoes, people praying
into morning. A fellowship of family
      slides Granddad into his burial house
      singing the old parish songs.

First Time in Jamaica

When I went to my mother's home,
it was the first time I touched Jamaican soil.
At nineteen I went to bury my grandfather

in the town of Bath. On this mountain
woven with trees of breadfruit, banana,
ackee, ambarella, plantain, pineapple,

pomegranate, guava, tamarind, coconut,
lychee, mango. Flavours my mummy would
climb for in her youth along the two-mile

walk of a rocky dirt road where driven
cars couldn't go. We knew the family
homes weren't far, hearing dominos

slamming, shaking tables, voices blending,
country dialect combing in chorus
this first day of Nine Nights. A slow

gathering of friends and family,
in nine nights to celebrate life of lost.

Lessons to Unprivileged

I tell my son
not to anger
at injustice—
teach him
to have a poker face—
bluff his emotions—
hide his gritting teeth,
cringing eyebrows—
relax his clinching fists,
not to react, but
to engage his eight-
year-old senses.

I tell my son
to observe
each environment
he enters, survey
the eyes probing him,
hearken the voices
murmuring his name—
connect personalities
to chess pieces—
predicting patterns
to employ
engaging tactics
to his ten-
year-old judgement.

I tell my son
society's first sight
of him has judgment—

a community's norms
paint him
as a thief—
trouble—threatening
in their schools,
jobs, neighborhoods—
prudence has me teach
him to dress sharp, smile
often, politely speak—
engaging opportunities,
through doors
choosing to slam shut.

Acknowledgments

Blessed acknowledgements are made to the following publications, in which some of these poems originally appeared:

"Manhood's Gambit" and "Chess Piece Patterns" in *AGNI*, "Stick, Hook, and a Pile of Yarn'" in *filling Station Magazine*, "Foreign Object" in *The Trinity Review*, "Lessons to Unprivileged" in *African American Review*, "Nine Months in Midwest Wheat Country" in *The Fourth River Literary Journal*, "Three Winters" in *The Cape Cod Poetry Review*, "A Man's Demons" in *Burningword Literary Journal*, "Nine Nights" in *Z-Publishing Kentucky's Best Emerging Poets 2019*, "Ice Pusher Cream Man" in *Rigorous Magazine*, "Each Time I Was Pulled Over, "and "First Time in Jamaica" *in Arlington Literary Journal*, "The Mushroom Cloud" in *Montana Mouthful*, "Stains of His Memory" in *The iō Literary Journal*, "First Highway Drive in America" in *Griffel Norwegian-English Literary Journal*, "An Unforgotten Path," "From Athens to Tellico, Tennessee," and "An Assault Rifle Ode" in *The Write Launch Literary Magazine*, "The Voice of Her Work," in *Cry of the Poor 2021 Anthology (*Culture Matters Ltd*)*, "Raggedy Rusted Fifteen-Year Old Red Car," in *Black Sunflower Poetry Press*, "Iceland, Her Touch of America," in *Round Table Literary Journal*, "Moments for a Legacy," in The Black Experience Anthology, "Ignorance Still Inherits Attention" in *Prometheus Dreaming Cultural Journal*.

* * *

I am very grateful to the creation of the Naslund-Mann Graduate School of Writing in Louisville, Kentucky to creators, and staff, Sena Naslund, Karen Mann, Kathleen Driskell, Lynnell Edwards, Katy Yocum, Jason Hill, and Ellyn Lichar. I especially give thanks to the mentor that saw me through the end and understood my writing to reach past appointed goals and farther for life, Douglas Manuel. I would also give appreciation to the mentors and assistance that provided fundamental grounding to be successful in this program Gregory Pape, Rachel Harper, Kathleen Driskell and Lynnell Edwards. It is due to this framework of fundamentals that work has been selected and published by so many well-known publications.

* * *

Most importantly it is necessary to give thanks and love to my amazing wife and son, Stephanie and Sioni Seivwright, who through this period provided the space, love, and support to stay focused, grounded, and committed to my path in writing.

* * *

Lastly, I hold this collection in memory of my amazing mum, Daphne Elora Guthrie, who never saw the path I chose, but I believe knew from the two inch Shakespearean Sonnet book she passed on to me along with the blanket that inspired this collection.

LAY OUT YOUR UNREST